Wandering
PARIS
with the artist Jill Butler

The
Globe
Pequot
Press

GUILFORD, CONNECTICUT

Text and illustrations: Jill Butler
Design: Jill Butler

Library of Congress Cataloging-in-Publication Data is available
ISBN 10: 0-7627-3804-9
ISBN 13: 978-0-7627-3804-5

Manufactured in Korea
First Edition/Second Printing

 ACKNOWLEDGMENTS

s a child I had a dream: I was on the Left Bank looking across the Seine to the backside of Notre-Dame. That image stayed with me. In 1979, I was looking for my first Paris apartment and I found my dream on the top floor of a former cloister directly across the street from Notre-Dame. The bells awakened me every morning, the tour buses kept me company on weekends, and I realized that dreams do come true!

I learned to love Paris by instinct and by following what appealed to me visually. I followed the addresses on endless posters for art exhibitions all over the city and rode the metro to the last stop on the line, where I descended and wandered. I pushed doors even when they looked closed and spoke terrible French until I didn't. With time, I made French friends who showed me their city.

To my friends of Paris, I thank you!

I am grateful to my clients, fans, and publisher, who allow me to draw and write about what I love. My coaches, Joe Rubin and Monica Landry, continue to keep me balanced and on the page.

Thank you to Mary Norris and Sarah Mazer, my adorable editors, who wouldn't let me not finish the book when I hit a health crisis midway. Tessa Wohl lent her artistic hand. Rebecca Russell showed infinite patience in her research. Aline Guillermain in Paris found the lost addresses of things I could see but not exactly remember.

And once again, with care and professionalism, Bob VanKeirsbilck pulled through another massive computer design project.

Thank you one and all for your love and support.

 # CONTENTS

Design Moments 1–3
Marvel at Paris' architectural wonders

A Water Day 4–11
See the city from the Seine, then relax at the beach

A Flea Market Expedition 12–17
Comb the best markets for treasures old and new

An Art Day 18–25
Take to the museums, or create your own masterpiece

An Arts and Crafts Day 26–27
Explore craft studios and boutiques in the Viaduc des Arts

The Canals of Paris 28–31
Float under the footbridges of the Canal Saint-Martin

Turning Water into Wine 32–37
Try a different wine every day

PARIS NEIGHBORHOODS

or *Arrondissements*, of which there are twenty.

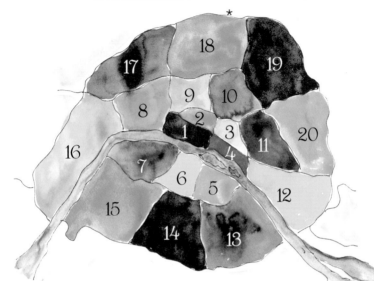

1
Louvre, Tuileries

3
Centre Pompidou,
Musée Picasso

4
Notre-Dame,
Hôtel de Ville,
Village St-Paul,
Paris Plage

5
Mosquée de Paris,
Jardin des Plantes,
Muséum d'Histoire
Naturelle

6
St-Germain,
Place Fürstemberg

7
Tour Eiffel,
Musée d'Orsay

8
Champs-Élysées,
Arc de Triomphe,
Marché des
Timbres,
Concorde,
Place Madeleine

9
Opéra, Garnier

10
Le Point Ephèmere

11
Bastille,
Canal Cruises

12
Opéra Bastille,
Viaduc des Arts,
Marché d'Aligre,
Gare de Lyon

13
Bibliothèque FR.
Mitterrand,
Scene-Est

15
Friday Skate,
Gare
Montparnasse,
Musée de la Poste

16
rue Passy,
Musée du Vin

18
Pigalle,
Monmartre, Sacré-
Coeur

19
Parc de la Villette

20
Père Lachaise
Cimetière

*Marché aux
Puces

Note: the 2nd,
14th, and 17th
arrondissements
are not repre-
sented in this
book.

 Introduction

Wandering … allowing time to stroll, meander, and experience moment by moment the details of life, art, and design.

You can be your own guide to discovering Paris. My intent is simply to offer ideas as a *point de départ,* point of departure—based on what you feel like seeing and doing that day. The French have a great word for this: to *flâner,* or to be a *flâneur,* **allowing natural curiosity to lead.**

Never decide what to do until after coffee. Check on the weather and your energy level. Maybe it's a day to spend on the river, or maybe your energy is way up there and you're ready for an adventure at the flea market, *marché aux puces.*

Take time to engage people even if you don't speak the language. Being quietly appreciative is the ultimate communication, as it comes from the heart, not from efforted language.

This book is not a checklist of must-sees or -dos. It's my insider's view, intended to whet your appetite for exploring my beloved, magical city. So *bon appétit!*

HOW TO USE THIS BOOK

 today I feel like ... is a reflection of your personal barometer

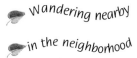 indicates something useful or interesting—an insider tip

 Wandering nearby

in the neighborhood

These are suggestions for monuments, museums, or points of interest to see while you're in the neighborhood.

The information icon signifies that there's an address, metro station, telephone number, or other useful information in the appendix, which starts on page 76. I've checked to make sure that the information is accurate, but of course some of the boutiques or restaurants mentioned may have closed. I apologize if you get disappointed.

 Maps are definitely not to scale, but are meant to give you a sense of the general area for your wandering. The maps at the start of each chapter are for that chapter's lead adventure. A "real" map will be useful.

Metro stations are noted either in the text or in the appendix.

 Throughout the book you will find illustrated vocabulary words, each with a simplified pronunciation. If all else fails, feel free to point—with a smile.

GETTING FROM A TO B

Walking is the best way to know the city. I always carry an extra pair of shoes for when my feet need a refresher.

The metro is the most efficient travel mode and can get you anywhere. The metro is totally user-friendly once you understand the basics. Pick up a free metro map from a ticket booth.

I love the bus, but using it is tricky if you don't know the city well. If you can get a direct bus, it's a pleasure to be aboveground. Consult the map and bus route posted at each stop. Metro tickets are valid.

Sometimes you just need to take a taxi. Either you can't walk another minute, time is of the essence, you're dressed to the hilt for dinner, or your destination is a bit out of reach. Taxis are expensive, as in every city … but then how often are you in Paris? Find a taxi station, *une tête de station,* or have someone call *un taxi* for you.

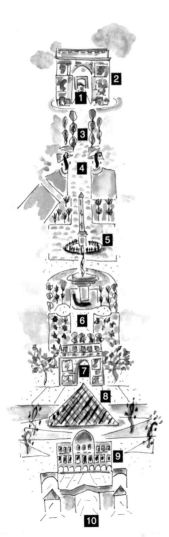

The Grand Alignment

1. Grande Arche de la Défense

2. Arc de Triomphe

3. Avenue des Champs-Élysées

4. Rond Point des Champs-Élysées
   The Stamp Market

5. Place de la Concorde

6. Jardin des Tuileries

7. Place du Carrousel

8. Pyramid du Louvre
   Cour Napoléon
   Café Marly

9. Cour Carrée

10. Rue de l'Amiral

DESIGN MOMENTS

Design waits to be appreciated in
the smallest and grandest details.

The Grand Alignment

Stand at one end of Paris at the Grande Arche de la Défense, or the other end, at the Pyramid du Louvre, and you will see what is called the Grand Alignment. It appears to have been created in one stroke of the brush—but not so. The line of buildings started with the brilliance of Baron Haussmann in 1853, and continued with the commissions of President François Mitterrand in the 1980s, creating the bookends of this remarkable spine.

While passing through the metro system, don't be in such a hurry to get to where you're going! Many design details and histories are on display here, as in the Louvre Station, line 1. I love the huge ads, billboards, and practical design solutions for seating (not sleeping). See if you can find the only two remaining original Art Nouveau entrances of architect Hector Guimard.

Note Take a look at the Concorde station, line 9, where the 1789 Bill of Rights is spelled out letter by letter in strikingly simple blue and white tiles.

un carnet = 10 metro tickets
uhn kahr•nay

la bouche de métro
lah boosh duh may•troh

Historically, Paris' newsstands, the Morris Column, street signs, book stalls, benches, and water fountains were painted in verdigris.

In 1982, for consistency of design and color, blue copper phtalocyanine and green chrome oxide were mandated for all street furnishings.

Note

A small river runs along the curb, making clean-up a fairly easy task.

3

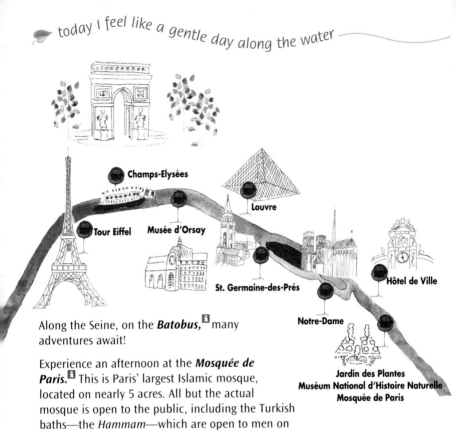

Champs-Elysées

Louvre

Tour Eiffel **Musée d'Orsay**

St. Germaine-des-Prés

Hôtel de Ville

Notre-Dame

Jardin des Plantes
Muséum National d'Histoire Naturelle
Mosquée de Paris

Along the Seine, on the **Batobus,** 🛈 many adventures await!

Experience an afternoon at the **Mosquée de Paris.** 🛈 This is Paris' largest Islamic mosque, located on nearly 5 acres. All but the actual mosque is open to the public, including the Turkish baths—the *Hammam*—which are open to men on Tuesday and Sunday and to women the other days of the week. Be sure to try the couscous restaurant, souk, and tearoom.

Wandering nearby

The gardens known as **Jardin des Plantes** 🛈 encompass the **Muséum National d'Histoire Naturelle** 🛈 (the Natural History Museum), an exceptional museum for all ages.

 A Water Day

*I like the Batobus—
a bus, taxi, and
sightseeing boat in one
that makes frequent stops
along the Seine.*

La Tour Eiffel
lah toor eh•fehl

L'Arc de Triomphe
lahrk duh tree•yohmf

BATOBUS

6

Notre-Dame
nuh•truh•dahm

Le Sacré-Coeur
luh sah•kray•kuhr

You can cruise by the major monuments, stay on the Batobus, or get off, wander, and return to the boat for the continuation of the itinerary.

Sometimes it's great just to go from one end of the city to the other on the water, watching the houseboats and river activity.

Check with the **Batobus** ⚅ for exact schedules and points of departure.

la Seine
lah sehn

The Wallace
Fountain from
1870 ensured
Parisians clean
drinking water.

Parisian fountains
are a delight—
and varied. See
how many you
can find through-
out the city.

Cour du Louvre

The Stravinsky Fountain, designed by Nikki St. Phalle and Jean Tinguely, is next to the **Centre Pompidou.** 🔢

A great view of old Paris may be had from the Pompidou terrace. It's free; just take the escalator to the top.

🍂 *Wandering nearby*

Dame Tartine 🔢 is a charming, relaxing *café* in front of the Stravinsky Fountain. What's a *tartine*? See page 20.

Within the Tuileries Garden is **Café Renard,** 🔢 an open greenhouse-style *café* located half-way along the *grande allée*.

RÉPUBLIQUE
FRANÇAISE   5,00

Postal stamp by Jean
Tinguely, 1988

You may think "water bars" must be a typo for wine bars ... not so!

The new champagne is WATER. The French say that their city water isn't safe to drink, and waiters encourage this notion as a way to sell more bottled water, *mais oui!* So why not *les bars d'eaux?*

While shopping the chic rue St-Honoré, check out **Colette,**  a trendy boutique with a water bar on the lower level. Hundreds of choices from around the world are available here, well beyond the better-known Nestlé brands such as Perrier, Poland Springs, and so on.

Note

Paris' drinking water is definitely safe to drink, if not chic. Don't be intimidated: Ask for *eau de ville,* city water. Drink lots of water on your flight; it will aid in getting over jet lag. Eight ounces are recommended for every hour of flying. Get an aisle seat! Hold off on the wine until you arrive in Paris.

A Day at the Beach

Here's a unique experience: Go to the beach along the Seine. The **Paris Plage** has a short season, but if your schedule brings you to Paris mid-July through mid-August, you'll find sand, palm trees, umbrellas, rollerblading, bikes, *pétanque*—plus a swimming pool for you and 200 other people. Great sightseeing, and novel to say the least.

Note

Efforts at lap swimming will not be successful.

Public swimming pools are abundant in Paris, and some are exceptional. My favorite is the historic **Piscine Pontoise,** located just across the Pont de l'Archeveche from the back end of Notre-Dame. Invariably, I'd meet other ex-pats doing laps and dodging the non-swimmers while thoroughly enjoying the 1930s architecture. The changing cabins are classic—160 of them border three sides of the 100-yard pool. It sure doesn't look like the YMCA of the USA! The Piscine Pontoise is open 'til 11:30 PM.

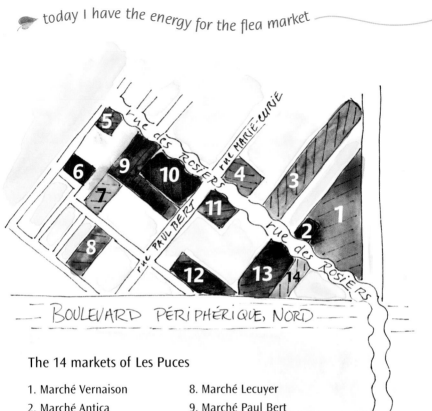

today I have the energy for the flea market

The 14 markets of Les Puces

1. Marché Vernaison
2. Marché Antica
3. Marché Biron
4. Marché Cambo
5. Marché L'Entrepot
6. Marché L'Usine
7. Marché J. Valles
8. Marché Lecuyer
9. Marché Paul Bert
10. Marché Serpette
11. Marché des Rosiers
12. Marché Malik
13. Marché Dauphine
14. Marché Malassis

A FLEA MARKET EXPEDITION

There's a fine art to finding
and collecting what some call junk
and others call treasures.

You could easily come to Paris and spend your entire trip at the flea market, **Marché aux Puces.**

Shop windows cover 17 acres, so get on your walking shoes and make sure this is a high-energy day. There are in fact 14 different markets, each with a distinctive ambiance and merchandise specialty.

Les Puces is open Friday and Monday 7 AM–1 PM, and Saturday and Sunday 10 AM–6 PM.

Take the metro, line 4, to the end—Porte de Clingancourt. Then follow the crowd. Three blocks under the highway, take a left onto rue des Rosiers, which is the principal street of the entire market.

Marché Vernaison is the first market along the rue des Rosiers. It's also the oldest of the markets, and definitely has the most authentic old village atmosphere. Stroll down the different alleys as more markets connect along the way, including:

The very appealing **Marché Serpette** and **Marché Paul Bert** sell garden and architectural elements.

Marché Biron is best for high-quality antiques.

Marché Dauphine has both antique books and glassware.

Note

For lunch, go to the Marché Vernaison and enjoy **Chez Louisette,** one of the highlights of a visit to the market. Crowd around a small table, eat, and hear an old-time *chanteuse* belt out Edith Piaf numbers accompanied by an accordion.

Nearby, **Le Saint Framboise** is a bit quieter, although the food is not exceptional.

A small detour at the
market for clothes, boots,
scarves, and souvenirs can
prove worthwhile.

If you still have shopping energy after a day at the flea market, get off the
metro, line 4, at station St-Germain-des-Prés and check out Monoprix.

Monoprix is a reasonably priced and surprisingly chic chain store with outlets all over the city. The stores are basic looking—but don't let looks deceive. Savvy Parisienne women buy their kids' clothes here and swear by the make-up offerings of the store brand Bourjois (which is apparently from the same factory as Chanel cosmetics). Look for trendy accessories, housewares, and a food market. One of the chain's largest stores is at the corner of Blvd. St-Germain-des-Prés and rue de Rennes.

"J'adore Monoprix."

✒ wandering nearby

Visit *l'Eglise St-Germain-des-Prés* or have a tea or an *apéritif* at **Café Les Deux Magots** on the Blvd. St-Germain.

un poudrier
uhn poor•dree•yay

le désodorisant
luh day•zoh•doh•ree•zahn

un rouge à lèvres
uhn rooj ah leh•vruh

un mascara
uhn mahs•kah•rah

une crème de visage
oon krehm duh
vee•zahj

l'eau de cologne
loh duh kuh•luhn•yuh

une crème de soleil
oon krehm duh suh•leh•yuh

une crème
oon krehm

17

La Palette
43, rue de Seine

4

AN ART DAY

Left Bank art dealers and students from the nearby École des Beaux-Arts hang out at La Palette.

STRONG COFFEE and early morning sketching

Start early with breakfast in the back room of *La Palette.*

Draw, sketch, write in a cozy banquette, drink strong coffee, and eat *croissants* or *tartines* smeared with butter and jam. The staff may be setting up for the day, but no one will bother you.

Here you can also experience a classic Greek version of *les toilettes*. This is not a shower room; the rest I'll let you figure out.

un cappuccino
uhn kah•poo•chee•noh

un thé...nature
uhn tay nah•toor

un chocolat chaud
uhn shuh•kuh•lah shoh

un café américain
uhn kah•fay
ameri•kehn

un express
uhn ehks•prehs

un croissant
uhn krwah•sahn

une tartine
oon tahr•teen

ART POSTERS lead the way

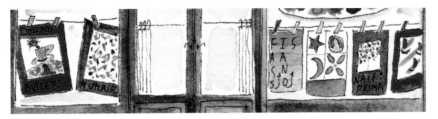

Flags, posters, and banners in every shop window announce exhibitions currently taking place in the city. The one that appeals to you is the one to follow. Take the metro, find your venue, and then wander the neighborhood, discovering Paris.

Note

If you lose your way, don't panic! There's a metro station every 2 to 3 blocks.

Wandering nearby

rue Jacob: lots of small boutiques
rue des Beaux Arts: art galleries
rue Buci: food market and *cafés*

rue Bonaparte: antique dealers; leads back to Blvd. St-Germain
rue de Seine: galleries; leads back to La Seine

In the Studio with the Artist

I like to see artists' work outside large museums, in more intimate settings such as **Atelier Brancusi,** 🔢 the sculpting studio of Constantin Brancusi. It is located next to the Centre Pompidou. 🔢

The **Musée Picasso** 🔢 is just a 15-minute walk from the Center Pompidou, not far from the Place des Vosges.

From 1887 until her death in 1926, the beloved American impressionist painter **Mary Cassatt** lived in Paris at 10, rue Marignan. Although this is a private residence, you can still wander by.

The **Atelier Delacroix** 🔢 is a museum and the artist's former residence on the Place Fürstemberg, not far from La Palette. 🔢

FOURNITURES POUR ARTISTES

The ancient manufacturer **Sennelier** 🗂 has a retail store with the world's finest pastels and other art materials.

Marie Papier 🗂 offers fashion-forward colored paper, novel notebooks, and gift wraps—a must!

Papier Plus 🗂 has the *crème de la crème* of handmade paper goods.

Some department stores have art departments.

Bon Marché 🗂 features a great selection of art supplies, paper goods, cards, and craft materials. While you're there check out the fresh food market.

BHV 🗂 offers a broad selection for the serious artist. The hardware department in the basement is also worth a look. Here, too, you'll find the Hôtel de Ville metro entrance.

la peinture
lah pehn•toor

les pinceaux
lay pehn•soh

un stylo
uhn stee•loh

les pastels
lay pahs•tehl

les aquarelles
layz ah•kwah•rehl

Musée de la Publicité 🛈
Advertising Museum

This is a personal favorite, located in the Musée Arts and Decoratifs of the Louvre. Advertising posters from the 1930s to 1960s by Cassandre (Bally shoes, Orangina, Perrier) and Savignac (Monsavon au Lait, BIC pens) are familiar, yet so graphically brilliant as to take your breath away. The collection consists of 50,000 pre–World War II posters and another 50,000 postwar posters—and growing. Exhibits change regularly.

🖋 *Wandering nearby*

Musée du Louvre 🛈

Les Arcades de rue de Rivoli

une affiche = a poster

Place des Vosges, the oldest square in Paris, boasts some of the priciest real estate in the city. Number six was once home to Victor Hugo, author of *Les Misérables.* It's open for visiting.

GALERIE D'ART

EXPOSITION
GUILLERMAIN
MARS 17

OUVERT
MARDI-SAMEDI
11h-19h

Not far from the Bibliothèque Nationale lies **Scene-Est de Paris,** a cutting-edge art gallery district. The galleries, which feature the conceptual and contemporary work of emerging artists, are open 2–7 PM.

Take the new high-tech, driverless metro, line 14, Bibliothèque FR. Mitterrand.

FAVORITES

_____
_____
_____
_____
_____
_____
_____
_____
_____
_____
_____

Note

Other art gallery districts:

Le Point Ephèmere 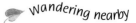 includes exhibit space, living spaces for artists, a restaurant, and a performance area. It's located along Canal Saint-Martin.

Around the **Centre Pompidou**

The **Left Bank** around La Palette

Wandering nearby

Visit the **Bibliothèque Nationale,** one of Mitterand's _grand projets._ _Mon dieu!_ What was Mitterrand thinking when he approved the four glass buildings resembling four open books? Of course rare books should not be exposed to direct sunlight … but that's exactly what was created. An inner lining of opaque wood is now in place to block the light and protect the precious contents.

The library is accessible to those who pay 3 euros. The fee may seem odd to some, but that's the way it is.

Viaduc des Arts 🔲 is an ancient railway viaduct hosting craft workshops, studios, and boutiques. To have history, creativity, and variety all in one location is a dream.

Take the metro to the Bastille and walk up avenue Daumesnil. There you will encounter the viaduct and its art galleries, craftsmen of all varieties, and the studios of such well-known designers as Phillippe Starck, Mourgue, and Wilmotte, to name a few.

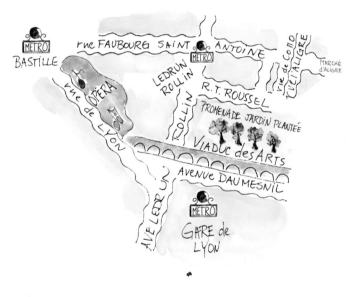

Fifty-six venues stretch for more than 2 blocks between metro Bastille and Gare de Lyon. On top of the viaduct is the **Promenade Plantée,** a spectacular walk that you should not miss.

The Promenade suspends you over the city like no place else in Paris … any one of the staircases will lead you up.

In one direction are the Bois de Vincennes, additional gardens, a cemetery, bike paths, and more. If you take this extended walk, bring a more detailed map. In the other direction, look for a stairway leading you back down to the Bastille metro. For a bite to eat, try the **Viaduc Café,** 🔲 open 8 AM–4 PM.

5

AN ARTS AND CRAFTS DAY

Finding great crafts in a unique locale makes for a double pleasure.

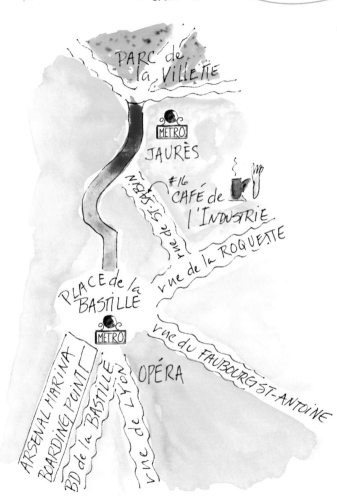

PARC de la VILLETTE

METRO JAURÈS

#16 CAFÉ de l'INDUSTRIE

rue de la ROQUETTE

rue de St SABIN

PLACE de la BASTILLE

METRO

rue du FAUBOURG ST-ANTOINE

ARSENAL MARINA BOARDING POINT

BD de la BASTILLE

rue de LYON

OPÉRA

The Canal Saint-Martin is the place to head when you're ready for a lovely water surprise. Here you can board a canal barge for a 2.5-hour cruise, ending at Parc de la Villette. The canal was featured in the 2001 movie *Amélie*.

6

THE CANALS OF PARIS

I love floating under the foot-bridges of the Canal Saint-Martin.

Cruising the **Canal Saint-Martin**[1]…

Near the Bastille metro station—across the street from 50, Blvd. de la Bastille—is the Arsenal Marina Boarding Point for the **Canauxrama.**[1] You can also start your cruise from the **Parc de la Villette**[1] and return to the Bastille.

Your cruise will take you past old working-class neighborhoods not yet gentrified, as well as unusual landscapes—it's quite irresistible. The canal is 2.8 miles long and has a water height difference of 82 feet, compensated for by a series of 9 locks, footbridges, and swing bridges.

Allow time to visit **Parc de la Villette,**[1] the largest green space in Paris, with 86 acres of lawns and gardens. Located at the edge of the city, the park mixes places for leisure activities, expositions, a science museum, and a geode, and it attracts millions of visitors every year.

To walk along the canal, you must start from metro République. Sadly, from the Bastille the canal is covered to create Boulevard Richard Lenoir.

Wandering nearby

For lunch before your cruise, try the cozy, hip **Café de l'Industrie,**[1] not far from the metro Bastille. It's off the beaten track and will take you into this neighborhood known for its woodworking *ateliers*—cabinet and furniture makers.

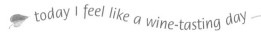

JACQUES MELAC
42 rue Léon Frot 11
01.43.70.59.27
BISTROT À VINS

rue LÉON FROT

rue de CHARONNE

METRO
CHARONNE

Every year a fresh *Beaujolais Nouveau* appears at the end of November and is greeted with great enthusiasm— particularly in the wine bars.

Beaujolais marks the beginning of the new wine season and is certainly cause for celebration.

7

TURNING WATER INTO WINE

*An opportunity to try
a different wine every day*

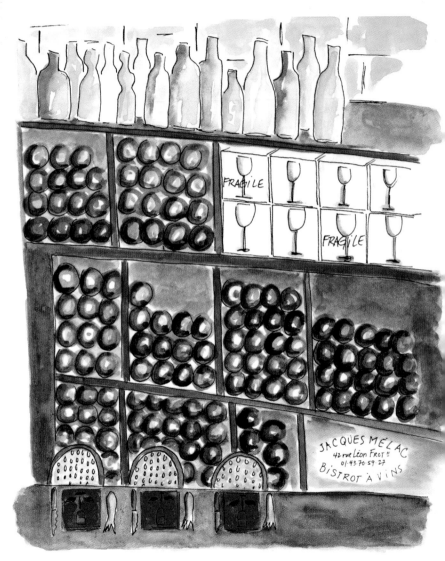

WATER INTO WINE

Jacques Melac,  one of my favorite *bistrot à vins*, is located in the Bastille area, metro Charonne.

This is a family affair, started by Jacques' father in the 1930s. Hundreds of wine bottles line the walls and create a fun, relaxed, unpretentious atmosphere. The bar is humming with activity. Simple, good food and a hearty welcome make for a relaxed neighborhood evening.

beaujolais
boh•juh•lay

bordeaux
bohr•doh

Note Jacques cannot imagine non-wine drinkers and has declared: *"Suite à la recrudesence des buveurs d'eau robinet et pour conjurer le mauvais sort la 2 ème carafe sera facturée 1 euro."* This translates to "Following the outbreak of drinkers of tap water and to ward off the unforgivable, the second pitcher (of water) will be billed at 1 euro."

une carafe d'eau
oon kah•rahf doh

chardonnay
shahr•duh•nay

Wandering nearby

Opéra de la Bastille  was destined to be the "people's opera." At best, its interior is reminiscent of a university lecture hall. Its claim to fame is the translation of all "foreign" lyrics, which are displayed in French on a huge digital *messagerie* above the stage. More distracting than useful.

Canal Saint-Martin (see page 28)

Charonne Food Market, open Tuesday and Sunday

un pichet (de vin)
uhn pee•shay (duh vehn)

bourgogne
boor•guhn•yuh

WINE BARS

Willi's Wine Bar, [i] a long-established, English-style wine bar, serves nice food at very small tables (generally with lots of smokers nearby). I like shopping in this neighborhood, around La Place Victoire.

You can find the absolute classic **Taverne Henri IV** [i] at the farthest point of the *cité*, where Notre-Dame is located. Those who come to drink here come daily—or perhaps several times a day. Who knows?

Verre Volé, [i] "the flying glass," is an itsy-bitsy wine bar with excellent food. It is located near Canal Saint-Martin, along the rue de Lancry, a street dotted with funky shops. Reservations are highly recommended.

Note 🌿

For shopping "by the bottle," visit the American-owned **La Dernière Goutte** [i] (The Last Drop), not far from the Place Fürstemberg.

LE TIRE-BOUCHON
BAR À VINS
26110 VINSOBRES, FRANCE

FONDÉE EN 1859
BEAUJOLAIS·VILLAGE
LOUIS JADOT
Beaune · France

CHÂTEAU
CHARONNE

WINES DISCOVERED

HOMAGE TO THE GRAPE

The **Montmartre Vineyard,** 🔢 Paris' only remaining vineyard, is not far from Sacré-Coeur and next to the famous cabaret **Au Lapin Agile.** 🔢 Every year on the first Saturday of October, there's a wine festival, *Fête du Vin,* with parades, music, and serious ceremony honoring the grape harvest.

Stamp by the artist Utrillo, who lived and worked here in his second-floor studio.

The picking of the grapes is done by City of Paris gardeners and park service workers. And the pressing of the grapes takes place in the *cave* of the Montmartre town hall. Seven hundred bottles of wine are produced from the ton of harvested grapes; a bottle can be purchased at the **Musée de Montmartre** 🔢 for roughly 35 euros. Proceeds of the wine sales go into the social services budget to benefit local residents.

I understand that the wine is rather undrinkable, but nobody seems to care. *Vive la tradition!*

Note

Take the *funiculaire* to the stop near Sacré-Coeur. 🔢 The train departs near Place St-Pierre.

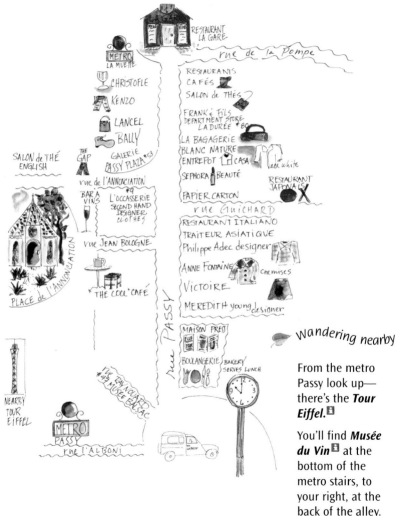

RESTAURANT LA GARE

METRO LA MUETTE

rue de la Pompe

CHRISTOFLE

KENZO

LANCEL

BALLY

THE GAP

GALERIE PASSY PLAZA *63

RESTAURANTS

CAFÉS

SALON de THÉS

FRANK & FILS DEPARTMENT STORE
LADURÉE *80

LA BAGAGERIE

BLANC NATURE

ENTREPOT CASA

abc white

SEPHORA BEAUTÉ

RESTAURANT JAPONAIS

PAPIER CARTON

SALON de THÉ ENGLISH

rue de l'ANNONCIATION

BAR A VINS

L'OCCASSERIE SECOND HAND DESIGNER CLOTHES

rue GUICHARD

RESTAURANT ITALIANO

TRAITEUR ASIATIQUE

Philippe Adec designer

ANNE FONTAINE chemises

rue JEAN BOLOGNE

"THE COOL" CAFÉ

VICTOIRE

MEREDITH young designer

PLACE de l'ANNONCIATION

rue PASSY

MAISON PREST

BOULANGERIE BAKERY SERVES LUNCH

NEARBY TOUR EIFFEL

rue FRANKLIN #47 MUSÉE BALZAC

METRO PASSY

rue l'ALBONI

LA POSTE

Wandering nearby

From the metro Passy look up—there's the **Tour Eiffel.**

You'll find **Musée du Vin** at the bottom of the metro stairs, to your right, at the back of the alley.

8

SHOPPING À LA PARISIENNE

"Just because I ignore you doesn't mean I don't want your business."

LE WEEKEND
MAGASIN de SPORT • RELAX • VOYAGE

Here you are on the **rue Passy,** in the heart of what's called the *seizième,* or 16th *arrondissement.* It's residential, upscale, and monied (yet under-stated), with designer boutiques, home furnishing shops, shoe stores, and small restaurants.

Another great shopping street frequented by *les Parisiennes* is **rue de la Pompe.** The neighborhood is full of young, cool, branded shops catering to students from the high school on rue de la Pompe—Lycée Jansen de Sailly.

Across from the high school is the well-known consignment shop **Réciproque.**  Designer labels and clothes with a history (if only they could talk!) are sold here at good prices. Black dinner dresses, sportswear, bags, and shoes are all available. There are also men's and children's shops.

For other types of bargain shopping, check out the book *Paris, pas Cher (Paris, not Expensive)*. It will give you lots of good ideas for finding clothing, home goods, and culinary supplies at reasonable prices.

En Soldes—On Sale

Some people go to Paris just for the season of *Les Soldes*. A 50 percent reduction is the norm during the major sale periods of mid-January through February and mid-July through August. During *Les Soldes* customers are known to line up outside the major designer boutiques very early in the morning. They are allowed to enter only as others depart.

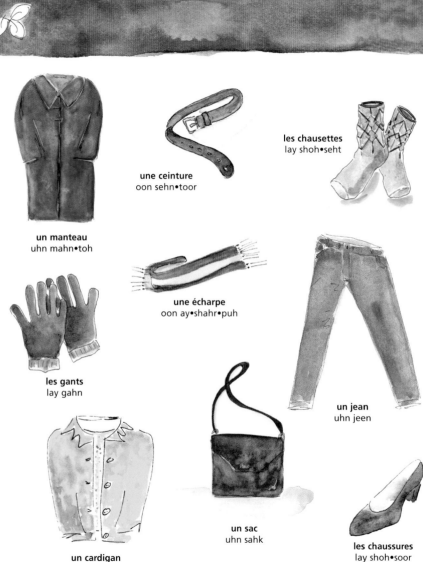

un manteau
uhn mahn•toh

une ceinture
oon sehn•toor

les chausettes
lay shoh•seht

les gants
lay gahn

une écharpe
oon ay•shahr•puh

un jean
uhn jeen

un cardigan
uhn kahr•dee•gahn

un sac
uhn sahk

les chaussures
lay shoh•soor

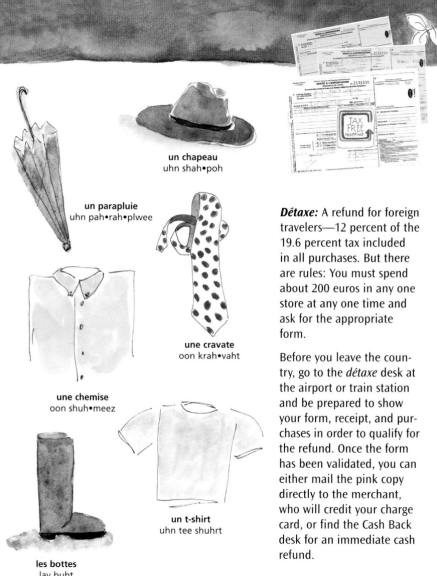

un chapeau
uhn shah•poh

un parapluie
uhn pah•rah•plwee

une cravate
oon krah•vaht

une chemise
oon shuh•meez

un t-shirt
uhn tee shuhrt

les bottes
lay buht

Détaxe: A refund for foreign travelers—12 percent of the 19.6 percent tax included in all purchases. But there are rules: You must spend about 200 euros in any one store at any one time and ask for the appropriate form.

Before you leave the country, go to the *détaxe* desk at the airport or train station and be prepared to show your form, receipt, and purchases in order to qualify for the refund. Once the form has been validated, you can either mail the pink copy directly to the merchant, who will credit your charge card, or find the Cash Back desk for an immediate cash refund.

It doesn't take much to be entertained in the City of Lights.

Paris is so stunningly beautiful by night that the sheer pleasure of being there is entertainment enough.

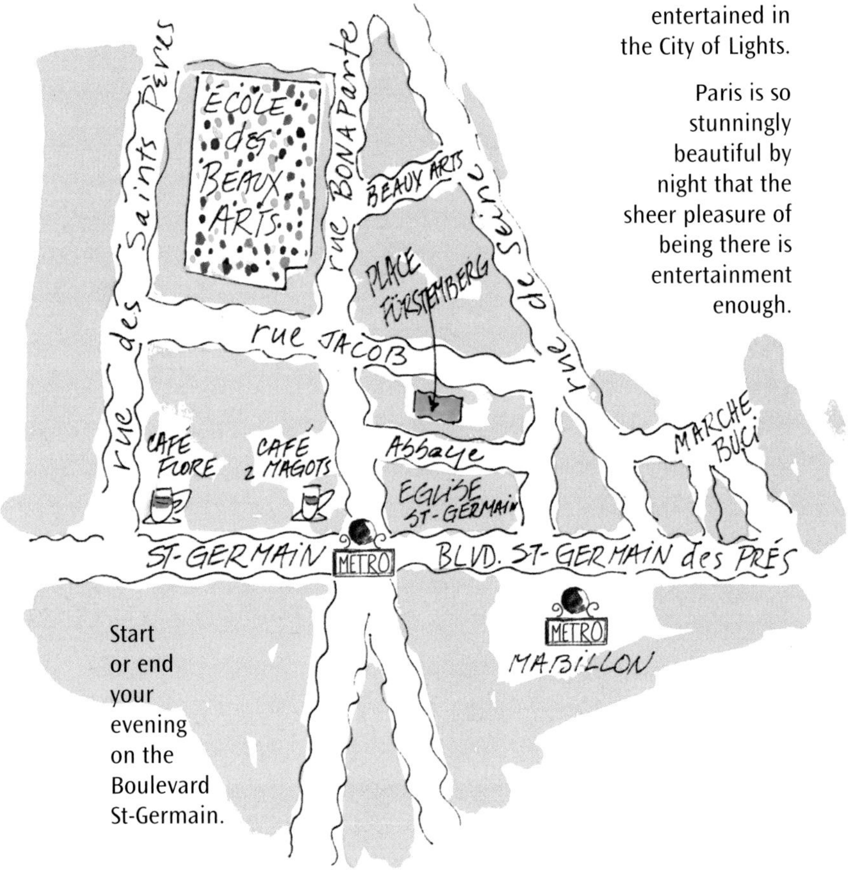

ÉCOLE des BEAUX ARTS

rue des Saints Pères

rue BONAPARTE

BEAUX ARTS

PLACE FÜRSTENBERG

rue de Seine

rue JACOB

MARCHE BUCI

CAFÉ FLORE

CAFÉ 2 MAGOTS

Abbaye

EGLISE ST-GERMAIN

ST-GERMAIN METRO BLVD. ST-GERMAIN des PRÉS

METRO MABILLON

Start or end your evening on the Boulevard St-Germain.

9

PARIS BY NIGHT

Cafés are both theater and audience. All life takes place here— or passes before it.

Café de Flore  and
Café Les Deux Magot
are ideal for
an evening of
people-watching.
Not only does
every type of person
walk by, but
the fire-eaters
and the
magicians
are more than
worth the price
of an *apéritif.*

The Place du Trocadéro is the ideal place to watch the Eiffel Tower flirt with you every hour, with its sparkling 10-minute light show. The lights, installed for the year 2000 celebration, have been such a hit that it seems they will stay forever.

For late night adventure, go to the top of Montmartre, on the terrace of **_Sacré-Coeur,_**  for a stunning view of Paris. When the monuments go dark, you're left with pin drops of light dabbled throughout the city—or maybe the last **_Bateaux-Mouches_** finding its way back to its berth.

Other nighttime opportunities:

The Friday Night Skate  Get on your knee pads and suit up for rollerblading by night on escorted journeys though the city. Skate dates are every Friday night—except when it rains or when the streets are wet. Skating starts at 10 PM and lasts 3 hours, returning to the starting point at 1 AM.

Make it an evening and visit the **Musée du Louvre** Wednesday or Friday night until 9:30 PM, then dine on the terrace at **Café Marly** (weather permitting), facing the Louvre on the Cour Napoléon looking directly at I.M. Pei's Pyramid. The evening lighting is superb. Reservations are highly recommended.

English-language movies are abundant at the **Champs-Elysées movie theatres.** Look for the letters V.O.—version original—meaning the film will be shown in the language in which it was created. Check *Pariscope,* found on every newsstand, for listings.

Tuesday through Sunday, you can visit **Le Palais de Tokyo** until midnight. What's inside? Contemporary art of the 20th century, from Henri Matisse to Pablo Picasso. Its manageable size and impressive art makes this one of my favorite museums—plus the simple restaurant serves until 11:30 PM.

Musée de l'Erotisme offers erotism in multiple art forms. Yes, it's unique! Open daily until 2 AM. Not surprisingly, this museum is located in the rather seedy Pigalle section, at the base of Montmartre.

Stamp by Bernard Buffet
Académie Française, 1978

10

WRITING HOME

Make this the day to send postcards. Friends and family will be thrilled.

France has a long tradition of honoring artists on stamps that are worth saving even if you're not a stamp collector. I use them in making collages.

Marché des Timbres, 🔲 the stamp market, is located off the Avenue des Champs-Elysées. Dealers hang the stamps in plastic pages organized by country or theme around the wall of their tents, or more seriously in stamp books. Don't touch the stamps; ask for tweezers to pick them up. Phone cards are also sold and traded at this market.

If you're inspired to write home, head for one of the best art postcard shops, *Cartes d'Art.* 🔲 Tourist postcards are less expensive, but buying artist-created cards is special and very French.

At the *Musée de la Poste,* 🔲 fans of "snail mail" can follow the transport of written communication by the French postal system.

The boutique offers related items.

THE POST OFFICE "ADVENTURE"

POSTCARDS TO SEND

Here is some useful vocabulary for buying stamps.

les timbres
lay tehm•bruh
stamps

les cartes postales
lay kahrt puhs•tahl
postcards

pour les Etats Unis
poor lays ay•tah•zoo•nee
for the United States

End your writing day at *Le Timbre*  with English chef Christopher Wright. Be sure to make a reservation, as it's the size of a postage stamp.

le bureau de poste
luh boo•roh duh puhst
post office

The post office is a multiservice center, so the lines may be long. To pass the time, look for the latest stamp editions displayed on a wall or ask to see them at the *Philadélique* window.

une boite aux lettres
oon bwaht oh leh•truh
mail box

Mail boxes are discreetly hung on the façades of buildings throughout the city.

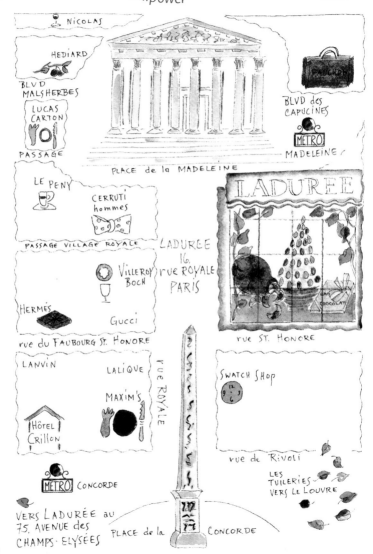

NICOLAS

HEDIARD

BLVD MALSHERBES

LUCAS CARTON

PASSAGE

PLACE de la MADELEINE

BLVD des CAPUCINES

METRO MADELEINE

LE PENY

CERRUTI hommes

PASSAGE VILLAGE ROYALE

LADUREE

LADUREE 16, rue ROYALE PARIS

VILLEROY BOCH

HERMÈS

Gucci

rue du FAUBOURG St. HONORE

rue St. HONORE

LANVIN

LALIQUE

MAXIM'S

rue ROYALE

SWATCH SHOP

Hôtel Crillon

rue de Rivoli

METRO CONCORDE

LES TUILERIES VERS LE LOUVRE

VERS LADURÉE au 75, AVENUE des CHAMPS-ELYSÉES

PLACE de la CONCORDE

11

BAKERY MOMENTS

Often I saw this fellow delivering bread in his own laid-back style ...

fresh every day and irresitible.

A *boulangerie* is a shop specializing in bread. A *patisserie* is a shop specializing in pastries, and it is often a *salon de thé* as well.

Both may carry bread *and* pasteries—but a shop's reputation is usually based on one or the other.

Ladurée 🔢 is a classic pastry shop and tea salon. Its specialty is macaroons (see map on page 56).

Paul, 🔢 the boulangerie, is a cousin to Ladurée. Paul shops are found throughout France and beyond.

Poujauran 🔢 is an award-winning bakery.

Pierre Hermé 🔢 hangs his reputation on his chocolate macaroons.

Poilâne 🔢 is a classic and the oldest bakery in France.

un croissant
uhn krwah•sahn

un pain de campagne
uhn pehn duh
kahm•pahn•yuh

un pain brioché
uhn pehn bree•yuh•shay

un palmier
uhn pahl•mee•yay

un pain aux raisins
uhn pehn oh reh•zehn

un pain aux olives
uhn pehn ohz uh•leev

une couronne
oon koo•ruhn

un pain aux noix
uhn pehn oh nwah

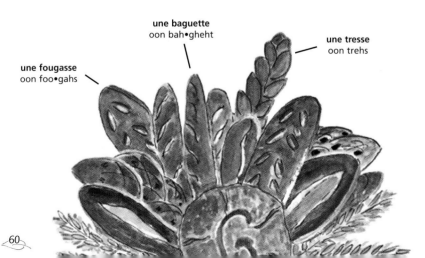

une baguette
oon bah•gheht

une tresse
oon trehs

une fougasse
oon foo•gahs

mado

While seated in **Ladurée** 🅸 on the rue Royale, look up at the ceiling and you will see angels baking the pastries and bread by the rays of the sun.

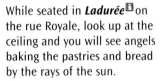

tarte aux fruits

Savarin

PÂTISSERIE
BOULANGERIE

PETITS PAINS

Ladurée sells some 12,000 of 20 or more varieties of its famous *macarons* daily.

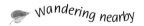

today I feel like some fresh air

The **Marché d'Aligre** 🔢 is the oldest, largest, and cheapest market in Paris. How's that for a recommendation?

On Sunday this place is very "in" with the in crowd and others. If crowds put you off, come on a weekday.

Marché d'Aligre map labels: BASTILLE METRO, rue FAUBOURG SAINT ANTOINE, rue de LYON, OPÉRA, LEDRUN ROLLIN METRO, ROLLIN, R.T. ROUSSEL, PROMENADE JARDIN PLANTÉE, VIADUC des ARTS, AVE LEDRU, Avenue DAUMESNIL, GARE de LYON, rue de COTTE, rue d'ALIGRE

MARCHÉ d'ALIGRE

Open daily, except Monday, 9 AM—1 PM.

Wandering nearby

Viaduc des Arts 🔢
Le Train Bleu 🔢
The Bastille area
Canal Saint-Martin 🔢

Find a *café* near the market and have breakfast. It's quite festive, and fun to people-watch.

In addition to all the foodstuffs, there's a flea market that dates back to the market's inception in the 13th century.

62

12

SLOW-DOWN SUNDAY

AVOCAT 4.50F   KIWI   ORANGE 12,40 K

FRUITS & PRIMEURS

GOLDEN 3,90 K   BANANE 13.K   TOMATE 12,90

LES FLEURS de MARIE-ANTOINETTE

*Marché d'Aligre,
the quintessential
Sunday market*

DANCING ON THE SEINE

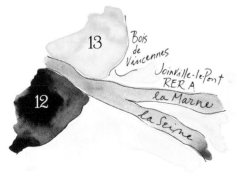

How I love the unexpected revival of things thought to be lost—like *les guinguettes* (gang-ETTE). These were, and are today, open-air restaurants, some on boats along the Seine and Marne Rivers. They offer the simple enjoyment of eating, drinking, and dancing to traditional accordion music. Here you step into a small corner of old-style Parisian life … like Renoir's *Luncheon of the Boating Party*. *Les guinguettes* are now fashionable with all ages. Enjoy Sunday afternoon dancing at ***Chez Gegene.***

A jog in the **Bois de Boulogne,** one of the most spectacular parks in Europe, is a very popular Sunday morning activity. You won't be alone.

Many **national museums** are free the first Sunday of the month.

From May through the end of July, a free **Jazz Festival** takes place on Saturday and Sunday in the Parc Floral de Vincennes, metro line 1, Château de Vincennes.

Every Sunday at 4:30 PM, a lovely free organ concert is offered at **Notre-Dame.** Afterwards, enjoy an ice cream at nearby **Maison Berthillon.**

On Sunday night it can be difficult to find a terrific restaurant that's open for dinner, other than in a good hotel. **Le Train Bleu,** in the Gare de Lyon, is my favorite. When making reservations, ask for a window seat. I love the view overlooking the trains arriving and departing, the weekenders returning, travelers scurrying to catch their trains, and the general hustle and bustle.

"I am 'le garçon' and I am in charge here."

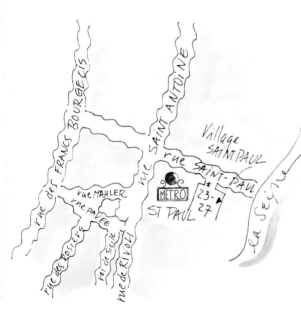

Village St. Paul,  an ancient village with mazes of court-yards and houses on different levels, is entirely occupied by galleries, bookstores, antiques dealers, and a few *cafés*. Meander in and out of the more than 60 *brocanteurs* and *antiquaires* gathered here.

This protected village is nestled behind some exceptional architecture in one of Paris' oldest districts, Le Marais, behind Hôtel de Ville (city hall).

🍃 *wandering nearby*

You're not far from:

The Seine

Musée Picasso 🛈

The Jewish quarter and the famous
Chez Jo Goldenberg 🛈

Shopping along **rue des Francs Bourgeois**

No matter what street you wander, you'll be discovering Old Paris.

If textiles are your thing, **Tissus Reine,** 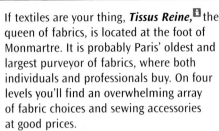 the queen of fabrics, is located at the foot of Monmartre. It is probably Paris' oldest and largest purveyor of fabrics, where both individuals and professionals buy. On four levels you'll find an overwhelming array of fabric choices and sewing accessories at good prices.

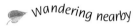 Wandering nearby

On the **Place Saint-Pierre** there are small trim shops, *les merceries,* for ribbons, buttons, and sewing accessories.

Also on the *Place* is **Halle Saint-Pierre,** with a restaurant, exhibition center, and the **Musée d'Art Naïf,** featuring the definitive collection of folk art paintings, including some by Grandma Moses.

I love buttons! If you do, too, be sure to visit **La Droguerie.** You'll also find beads, yarns, and great ideas for your projects.

Nearby are two hotel and restaurant supply shops for the cooking enthusiast: **E. Dehillerin** (Julia Child's favorite) and **A. Simon,** famous for glassware and more.

Wandering nearby

The **Forum des Halles,** an underground shopping center, is recommended for rainy days only.

Note

la batterie de cuisine = pots and pans, a restaurant supply store

On the Place Fürstemberg, nestled between rue Jacob and l'Abbaye St-Germain-des-Prés, are the home furnishing showrooms of some of Paris' top textile designers, such as *Pierre Frey* and *Manuel Canovas.*

You can walk into most showrooms and take notes on the fabrics you see. But you usually cannot buy on the spot, as the showrooms are for decorators and their clients.

However, I've been able to order these fabrics back home in the U.S.

Note 🍃

In the evening, the Place Fürstemberg is one of the most romantic spots in Paris.

69

BLVD. HAUSSMANN
#80
LA VAISELLERIE

rue TRONCHET

BISTROT
#34 POT au FEU
#24 MAISON du MIEL

#21 FERME ST HUBERT

#16 SAPONIFERE

HÉDIARD

FAUCHON

FAUCHON

FAUCHON

HABITAT
MAISON du CHOCOLAT

rue Boissy d'ANGLAS

TERRITOIRE

LUCAS CARTON

PARFUMERIE

PASSAGE MADELEINE

METRO
PLACE de la MADELEINE

BD de MADELEINE

OPÉRA

TERRITOIRE GIFTS!

CAFÉ LE PENY

VILLEROY-BACH

GUCCI

LE VILLAGE MADELEINE

rue ROYALE

MAILLE MOUTARDE

RALPH LAUREN

LADURÉE PATISSERIE

Wandering nearby

LALIQUE
CHRISTOFLE

HERMÈS

FAUBOURG ST. HONORÉ

rue ST. HONORÉ

SWAROSKI

MAXIMS

HÔTEL de CRILLON

METRO
CONCORDE

SWATCH WATCH

JOAILLERIE

When nature calls, visit *Les Toilettes Publiques in the Madeleine metro station.

The tile work is exceptional, and the individual stalls have polished dark wood doors.

There is even an attendant to assist you.

GIFTS FOR THE SUITCASE

Mustard takes on haute cuisine status.

FOOD AS GIFTS

Fauchon offers a feast in presentation of all kinds of packaged and freshly prepared foods.

Gifts from Fauchon are highly recognizable and will certainly be appreciated.

There's no better place to shop for mustard, *la moutarde,* than at the ***Maille Boutique*** on the Place de la Madeleine. Freshly prepared house blends and preservative-free mustards are available for tasting. Prepackaged varieties are also available. Maille mustard is a great Dijon mustard and a unique French gift.

Chocolate! Chocolate! Never enough chocolate! If you're invited to dinner or for the weekend at a French person's home, bring chocolate. Hands down, this is the gift of choice.

While you're on the Place de la Madeleine, make your way around the church to ***Hédiard*** for British specialties, especially teas and biscuits. Upstairs is a lovely restaurant for breakfast, lunch, or dinner.

In a totally different neighborhood, but worth the trip, is ***Mariage Frères.*** Four hundred varieties of tea are available at this ancient tea shop. The tea salon is elegant.

Never, ever, bring wine. You'll insult your host's wine cellar, and besides, what do we know about wine?

Needless to say, chocolate is also a great gift to take home.

La Maison du Chocolat is a terrific shop, as is ***La Fontaine du Chocolat.*** I love the *chocolat* flowing in the window fountain.

Behind Fauchon on the rue Vignon is **Saponifere.** 🔢 It has wonderful soaps and bath accessories appropriate as gifts.

Hidden and waiting to be discovered inside the Passage Madeleine is a snack bar, a floral designer, a wine merchant, and a personal favorite for gifts, **Territoire.** 🔢

These may be expensive—but less expensive if purchased in France! Don't forget about the *détaxe* (page 43).

Parfumerie 🔢

Lalique 🔢

Christofle 🔢

Hermès 🔢

LA VAISSELLERIE 🔢

This "dish seller" is a small boutique with a huge selection that spills onto the street. Culinary porcelain, ceramics, butter dishes, *escargot* plates, placemats, pitchers, and *hors d'oeuvres* sets are *une bonne affaire,* a good buy at a good price.

The bee—Napoléon's imperial crest—was and still is embroidered on all types of home furnishings, textiles, and robes. Glassware, dinnerware, and tabletop accessories also feature the bee.

To know more about these imperial bees, visit the *Musée de Notre-Dame-de-Paris.* [i] I used to live next door to this museum, on the charming rue du Cloître-Notre-Dame (the cloisters of Notre Dame).

La Maison du Miel, [i] the Honey House, offers an extensive selection of honey products. I appreciate this completely understated and simple old-style boutique.

The French particularly love honey, and it is marketed extensively. This is also a good house gift when invited overnight.

Bees live in Paris by the thousands—in beehives in the upper reaches of the *Opéra, Palace Garnier.* [i]

Due to the added warmth and abundance of floral material, the bees are said to be more productive here than in nature.

You can buy the honey harvested at the Opéra in its boutique, and at *Fauchon.* [i]

APPENDIX

A. Simon 68
destination   page number
36, rue Étienne Marcel, 2nd
street #, address, and arrondissement
Tel: 01 42 33 71 65
must use 01 in Paris
Mo: Étienne Marcel, line 4
metro station name, metro line #

Atelier Brancusi 21
Located outside Centre Pompidou
Open daily (except Tuesday) 2 - 6 PM

Atelier Delacroix 21
Musée Eugène-Delacroix
6, rue de Fürstemberg, 6th
Tel: 01 44 41 86 50
Mo: St-Germain-des-Prés, line 4
Closed Tuesday

Bateaux-Mouches 49
Pont de l'Alma
Right Bank, 8th
Tel: 01 42 25 96 10
www.bateaux-mouches.fr
Mo: Alma-Marceau, line 9
Schedule varies by season
Departures 10 AM - 11 PM

Batobus 4-7
Tel: 01 44 11 33 99
www.batobus.com
Tickets can be purchased at each stop.

BHV 22
Bazar de l'Hôtel de Ville
52, rue Rivoli, 4th
Tel: 01 42 74 90 00
Mo: Hôtel de Ville, line 1,11

Bibliothèque Nationale 25
11, quai François Mauriac, 13th
Tel: 01 53 79 59 59
www.bnf.fr
Mo: Bibliothèque FR Mitterrand, line 14

Bon Marché 22
24, rue Sèvres, 7th
Tel: 01 44 39 80 00
Mo: Sèvres Babylon, line 10,12

Café Les Deux Magots 17, 47
170, Blvd. St-Germain-des-Prés, 6th
Tel: 01 45 48 55 25
Mo: St-Germain-des-Prés, line 4

Café de Flore 47
172, Blvd. St-Germain-des-Prés, 6th
Tel: 01 45 48 55 26
Mo: St-Germain-des-Prés, line 4

Café de l'Industrie 31
16, rue St-Sabin, 11th
Tel: 01 47 00 13 53
Mo: Bastille, line 1,5,8
Closed Saturday

Café Marly 51
93, rue de Rivoli, 1st
Tel: 01 49 26 06 60
Mo: Louvre Palais Royal, line 1

Café Renard 9
Jardin des Tuileries, 1st
Tel: 01 42 96 50 56
Mo: Concorde, line 1,8

Canal St-Martin 28-31, 62
Canauxrama
50, Blvd. de la Bastille, 12th
Tel: 01 42 39 15 00
www.canauxrama.com
Mo: Bastille, line 1,5,8
Return via Jaurès, line 2,5,7
Departs approximately 9:45 AM and 2:30 PM
from both the Arsenal Marina and Parc de
la Villette

Canovas, Manuel 69
6, rue de l'Abbaye
St-Germain-des-Prés 6th
Tel: 01 40 51 95 30
Mo: St-Germain-des-Prés, line 4

Cartes d'Art 54
9, rue Dragon, 6th
Tel: 01 42 22 86 15
Mo: St-Germain-des-Prés, line 4

Centre Pompidou 9, 25
Place Georges Pompidou
rue Saint Martin, 4th
Tel: 01 44 78 12 33
www.cnac-gp.fr
Mo: Rambuteau, line 3,4;
Hôtel de Ville, line 1,7
Open daily (except Tuesday) until 9 PM

Chez Gegene 64
162 bis, Quai de Polangis
Joinville-le-Pont on the Marne River
6 miles east of Paris
Tel: 01 48 83 29 43
RER A: Joinville-le-Pont + 15-min. walk
Open April to mid-December
Lunch and dinner Friday, Saturday, Sunday

Chez Jo Goldenberg 66
7, rue des Rosiers, 4th
Tel: 01 48 87 20 16
Mo: St. Paul, line 1
Reservations a must!

Chez Louisette 15
Marché aux Puces
Marché Vernaison
130, ave Michelet
Tel: 01 40 12 10 14
Mo: Porte de Clingancourt, line 4

Christofle 73
9, rue Royale, 8th
Tel: 01 55 27 99 13
Mo: Concorde, line 1

Colette 10
213, rue St-Honoré, 1st
Tel: 01 55 35 33 90
Mo: Tuileries, line 1,7

Dame Tartine 9
2, rue Brise Miche, 4th
Tel: 01 42 77 32 22
Mo: Hôtel de Ville, line 1,7

E. Dehillerin 68
18-20, rue Coquillière, 1st
Tel: 01 42 36 53 13
Mo: Étienne Marcel, line 4;
Louvre Rivoli, line 1
Open daily (except Sunday) 8 AM - 6 PM;
limited hours Monday and in August.

La Dernière Goutte 36
6, rue Bourbon Le Château, 6th
Tel: 01 43 29 11 62
Mo: Mabillon, line 10;
St-Germain-des-Prés, line 4

La Droguerie 68
9, rue du Jour, 1st
Tel: 01 45 08 93 27
Mo: Étienne Marcel, line 4;
Louvre Rivoli, line 1

Fauchon 72, 75
26-30, Place de la Madeleine, 8th
Tel: 01 47 42 60 11
www.fauchon.com
Mo: Madeleine, line 8,12,14;
Concorde, line 1

La Fontaine du Chocolat 72
201, rue St- Honoré, 1st
Tel: 01 42 44 11 66
Mo: Tuileries, line 1

Forum des Halles 68
Porte Berger, 1st
Tel: 01 44 76 96 56
Mo: Les Halles, Châtelet, line 1,4,7,11
Open daily (except Sunday) 10 AM - 7:30 PM

Frey, Pierre 69
2, rue Fürstemberg, 6th
Tel: 01 43 26 82 61
Mo: St-Germain-des-Prés, line 4

Friday Night Skate 51
Place Raoul Dautry, 15th
www.pari-roller.com
Mo: Montparnasse, line 6,12,13
Friday at 10 PM, except when it rains or the streets are wet

Halle Saint-Pierre 68
2, rue Ronsard, 18th
Tel: 01 42 58 72 89
Mo: Anvers, line 2
Open 10 AM - 6 PM

Hédiard 72
21, Place de la Madeleine, 8th
Tel: 01 43 12 88 88
www.hediard.fr
Mo: Madeleine, line 8,12,14;
Concorde, line 1

Hermès 73
24, rue du Faubourg St- Honoré, 8th
Tel: 01 40 17 47 17
www.hermes.com
Mo: Concorde, line 1

Jardin des Plantes 4
rue Cuvier, 5th
Tel: 01 40 79 56 01
Mo: Jussieu, line 7,10

Ladurée 59, 61
16, rue Royale, 8th
Tel: 01 42 60 21 79
www.laduree.fr
Mo: Madeleine, line 8,12,14;
Concorde, line 1

Lalique 73
11, rue Royale, 8th
Tel: 01 53 05 12 12
Mo: Concorde, line 1

Au Lapin Agile 37
22, rue Saules, 18th
Tel: 01 46 06 85 87
Mo: Lamarck-Caulaincourt, line 12

Maille Boutique 72
6, Place de la Madeleine, 8th
Tel: 01 40 15 06 00
www.maille.com
Mo: Madeleine, line 8,12,14;
Concorde, line 1

Maison Berthillon 65
29-31, rue Saint-Louis-en-l'île, 4th
Tel: 01 43 54 31 61
Mo: Hôtel de Ville, line 1

La Maison du Chocolat 72
8, Blvd. Madeleine, 9th
Tel: 01 47 42 86 52
Mo: Madeleine, line 8,12,14;
Concorde, line 1

La Maison du Miel 75
24, rue Vignon, 9th
Tel: 01 47 42 26 70
Mo: Madeleine, line 8,12,14;
Havre Caumartin, line 3,9

Marché d'Aligre 62
Along rue and Place d'Aligre, 12th
Mo: Ledru-Rollin, line 8;
Bastille, line 1,5,8

Marché aux Puces 12-15
rue des Rosiers
Mo: Porte de Clingancourt
(end of the line), line 4.
Open Friday and Monday 7 AM - 1 PM
Saturday and Sunday 10 AM - 6 PM
Maps and info: www.vernaison.com
Guided tours, shipping assistance:
www.findsinparis.com

Marché des Timbres 54
Avenue Matignon, 8th
Mo: Franklin D. Roosevelt, line 1,9
Open Thursday, Saturday, Sunday, holidays
9 AM - 7 PM

Mariage Frères 72
30, rue du Bourg-Tibourg, 4th
Tel: 01 42 72 28 11
www.mariagefreres.com
Mo: Hôtel de Ville, line 1,11

Marie Papier 22
26, rue Vavin, 6th
Tel: 01 43 26 46 44
www.mariepapier.fr
Mo: Vavin, line 4;
Notre-Dame des-Champs, line 12

Melac, Jacques 35
Bistrot à Vins
42, rue Leon Frot, 11th
Tel: 01 43 70 59 27
www.melac.fr
Mo: Charonne, line 9

Monoprix 16-17
50, rue de Rennes, 6th
Tel: 01 45 48 18 08
Mo: St-Germain-des-Prés, line 4

Montmartre Vineyard 37
Corner of rue des Saules
and rue Saint Vincent, 18th
Mo: Anvers, line 2

Mosquée de Paris 4
2, bis Place du Puits de l'Ermite, 5th
Tel: 01 45 35 97 33
Mo: Jussieu, line 7,10

Musée d'Art Naïf 68
Halle Saint-Pierre
2, rue Ronsard, 18th
Tel: 01 42 58 72 89
Mo: Anvers, line 2
Open 10 AM - 6 PM

Musée de l'Erotisme 51
72, Blvd. de Clichy, 18th
Tel: 01 42 58 28 73
Mo: Blanche, line 2

Muséum National d'Histoire Naturelle 4
rue Geoffroy-St-Hillaire and
rue Buffon, 5th
Tel: 01 40 79 30 00
Mo: Jussieu, line 7,10

Musée du Louvre 23, 51
Pyramide-Cour Napoléon, 1st
Tel: 01 40 20 51 51
Mo: Louvre Palais Royal, line 1,7
www.louvre.fr
Open Monday, Thursday, Saturday, and Sunday 9 AM - 6:45 PM
Wednesday and Friday until 9:45 PM

Musée de Montmartre 37
12, rue Cortot, 18th
Tel: 01 46 06 61 11
Mo: Pigalle, line 2, walk up
or take funicular
Open daily (except Monday) 11 AM - 6 PM

Musée de Notre-Dame-de-Paris 75
10, rue du Cloître Notre-Dame, 4th
Tel: 01 43 25 42 92
Mo: Hôtel de Ville, line 1

Musée Picasso 21, 66
5, rue Thorigny, 3rd
Tel: 01 42 71 25 21
Mo: St-Paul, line 1;
Chemin Vert, line 8
Closed Tuesday

Musée de la Poste 54
34, Blvd. de Vaugirard, 15th
Tel: 01 42 79 24 24
Mo: Montparnasse, line 6,12,13
Closed Sunday

Musée de la Publicité 23
Les Arts Decoratifs/Louvre
107, rue de Rivoli, 1st
Tel: 01 44 55 57 50
www.lesartsdecoratifs.fr
Mo: Louvre Palais Royal, line 1,7

Musée du Vin 38
rue des Eaux, 16th
Tel: 01 45 25 63 26
Mo: Passy, line 6
Closed Monday

Notre-Dame 65
Place de Notre-Dame, 4th
Mo: Cité, line 4

Opéra de la Bastille 35
Place de la Bastille, 12th
Tel: 01 44 73 13 99
Mo: Bastille, line 1,5,8

Opéra, Palais Garnier 75
8, rue Scribe, 9th
Tel: 01 40 01 17 89
Mo: Opéra, line 3,7,8

Le Palais de Tokyo 51
13, Avenue du Président Wilson, 16th
Tel: 01 47 23 54 01
Mo: Iéna, line 6
Open daily (except Monday) noon - midnight

La Palette 20
43, rue de Seine, 6th
Tel: 01 43 26 68 15
Mo: St-Germain-des-Prés, line 4
Closed Sunday and August

Papier Plus 22
9, rue Pont Louis Philippe, 4th
Tel: 01 42 77 70 49
Mo: Hôtel de Ville, St-Paul, line 1

Parc de la Villette 31
Tel: 01 40 03 75 75
www.villette.com
Mo: Porte de Pantin, Ourcq, line 5

Parfumerie 73
La Beauté Internationale
26, Place de la Madeleine, 8th
Tel: 01 42 66 47 00
Mo: Madeleine, line 8,12,14;
Concorde, line 1

Paris Plage 11
Along the Right Bank,
near the Pont Neuf and Hôtel de Ville
Mo: Hôtel de Ville, line 1
Open 9:30 AM - 11 PM

Paul 59
37, rue Tronchet, 8th
Tel: 01 40 17 99 54
www.paul.fr
Mo: Havre-Caumartin, line 3,9
More than 30 locations in Paris

Pierre Hermé 59
72, rue Bonaparte, 6th
Tel: 01 43 54 47 77
Mo: Saint-Sulpice, line 4

Piscine Pontoise 11
18, rue Pontoise, 5th
Tel: 01 55 42 77 88
Mo: Maubert-Mutualité, line 10

Poilâne 59
8, rue du Cherche-Midi, 6th
Tel: 01 45 48 42 59
www.poilane.fr
Mo: Saint-Sulpice, line 4

Le Point Ephèmere 25
200, Quai de Valmy, 10th
Tel: 01 40 34 02 48
Mo: Louis Blanc, line 5,7

Poujauran 59
20, rue Jean Nicot, 7th
Tel: 01 47 05 80 88
Mo: La Tour-Maubourg, line

Réciproque 41
95, rue de la Pompe, 16th
Tel: 01 47 04 30 28
Mo: Rue de la Pompe, line 9

Le Saint Framboise 15
Marché aux Puces
142, rue des Rosiers, 2nd floor
Marché Malassis
Tel: 01 40 11 27 38
Mo: Porte de Clingancourt, line 4

Sacré-Coeur 37, 49
35, rue de Chevalier-de-la-Barre, 18th
Mo: Pigalle, line 2,12 + Montmartrobus;
Abbesses, line 12 + funicular

Saponifere 73
16, rue Vignon, 9th
Tel: 01 42 65 90 79
Mo: Madeleine, line 8,12,14;
Havre Caumartin, line 3,9

Scene-Est de Paris 24
rue Louise-Weiss, 13th
Mo: Bibliothèque FR Mitterrand, line 14;
Chevaleret, line 6

Sennelier 22
3, quai Voltaire, 7th
Tel: 01 42 60 72 15
www.magasinsennelier.com
Mo: Palais Royal, line 1,7, cross the river;
Rue du Bac, line 12

Taverne Henri IV 36
13, Place du Pont Neuf, 1st
Tel: 01 43 54 27 90
Mo: Cité, line 4;
Pont Neuf, line 7, cross the bridge

Territoire 73
30, Boissy d'Anglas, 8th
Tel: 01 42 66 22 13
Mo: Madeleine, line 8,12,14;
Concorde, line 1

Le Timbre 55
3, rue Sainte-Beuve, 6th
Mo: Notre-Dame-des-Champs, line 12
Tel: 01 45 49 10 40
Closed Saturday for lunch and Sunday

Tissus Reine 68
3-5, Place Saint-Pierre, 18th
Tel: 01 46 06 02 31
Mo: Anvers, line 2;
Abbesses, line 12

Tour Eiffel 38
www.tour-eiffel.fr
Mo: Champ de Mars/Tour Eiffel,
Passy, line 6
*Open daily year-round; hours vary
by season*

Le Train Bleu 62, 65
Gare de Lyon
Place Louis Armand, 12th
Tel: 01 43 43 09 06
www.le-train-bleu.com
Mo: Gare de Lyon, line 1,14

La Vaissellerie 73
80, Blvd. Haussmann, 8th
Tel: 01 45 22 32 47
Mo: Havre Caumartin, line 3,9

Verre Volé 36
67, rue de Lancry, 10th
Tel: 01 48 03 17 34
Mo: Jacques Bonsergent, line 5

Viaduc des Arts 26, 62
9-147, avenue Daumesnil, 12th
Tel: 01 44 75 80 66
Mo: Bastille, line 1,5,8;
Gare de Lyon, line 1,14
*Each store operates independently
In general, open Monday - Saturday
10 AM - 7 PM*

Viaduc Café 26
43, avenue Daumesnil, 12th
Tel: 01 44 74 70 70
Mo: Bastille, line 1,5,8;
Gare de Lyon, line 1,14

Village St. Paul 66
23-27, rue St-Paul, 4th
Mo: St-Paul, line 1
Open Thursday - Monday 11 AM - 7 PM

Willi's Wine Bar 36
13, rue des Petits Champs, 1st
Tel: 01 42 61 05 09
www.williswinebar.com
Mo: Bourse, line 3

Souvenirs de Paris

Note www.jillbutler.com

Soup/Salad Bowl
...I am "Le Monsieur" and I am in charge here

Salad Plate
...taking the time to watch the world go by

Tidbit Dishes
...try a different one every day

Dish Towel

Dinner Plate
...now I know I'm in Paris

Every drawing is a story told with few words. By drawing what I see, I never forget.

Souvenirs de Paris Collection of dinnerware by the piece, glassware, placemats, coasters and dish towels. Available at quality retailers and online at **www.jillbutler.com**

Coasters

Glassware

THE VILLAGE MERCHANTS... à vôtre service

Pasta/Soup Bowl

Dinner Plate

Salad Plate

Dinnerware by the piece, pasta bowls, and tidbit dishes feature some of my favorite storefronts.

LA POTAGERIE... the vegetable garden

"On the weekends in Normandy, we grew every kind of vegetable. Well, I didn't grow them, but I did paint them."

Pasta/Soup Bowl

Dinner Plate

Salad Plate

Tidbit Dishes

Dish Towels

Placemats

The Vegetable Garden Collection of dinnerware by the piece, glassware, placemats, coasters, and dish towels. Available at quality retailers and online at **www.jillbutler.com**

Rendez-vous with FRANCE

makes you comfortable and helps dispel your fears about not speaking the language. You don't have to know it all. Point! Pronounce! Play!

1,000 illustrations of everything you'll need to know for traveling, shopping, and eating. 60 pages of food, insider tips, and simplified pronunciation make it fun to pronounce or point for survival.

Wandering PARIS

gets you on the path to adventures and discovery in this incredible city.

The two together are a natural fit: one for survival, one for adventure.